CW00429533

Easy Italian Trav
Size Phrase book

Beginners Italian Phrase Book for
Travelers of Italy with a Broad Range of
Everyday Italian Phrases.

Marco Lorenzo

Copyright ©

Marco Lorenzo

© 2023 Italy

Table of Content

Introduction

Whether you're planning a leisurely vacation in the stunning cities of Italy or embarking on a business trip to this beautiful country, this pocket-sized phrase book is your essential companion for navigating the Italian language and culture with ease.

Italy, known for its rich history, captivating art, delectable cuisine, and warm-hearted people, offers an unforgettable experience to travelers from all around the world.

However, communicating effectively in a foreign language can sometimes be challenging and intimidating.

That's where this phrase book comes in handy, equipping you with the essential phrases and expressions needed to bridge the language gap and enhance your travel experience.

Designed specifically for travelers, this compact and user-friendly phrase book is conveniently sized to fit into your pocket, making it easily accessible whenever you need it.

Whether you're strolling through the charming streets of Rome, exploring the artistic wonders of Florence, or indulging in the romantic ambiance of Venice, this book will serve as your linguistic companion, helping you navigate various situations encountered during your journey.

Inside these pages, you'll find a comprehensive collection of practical phrases and expressions carefully selected to meet the needs of travelers.

Starting with the basics, you'll learn essential greetings and introductions, polite expressions, and common phrases for asking for help and directions. The book then guides you through various travel scenarios such as getting around, accommodations, dining out, shopping, entertainment, and emergencies, providing you with the necessary vocabulary and phrases specific to each situation.

Additionally, this phrase book offers insights into Italian culture and etiquette, enabling you to interact with locals in a respectful and friendly manner.

You'll find tips on restaurant etiquette, bargaining, and engaging in small talk, ensuring you connect with the Italian people on a deeper level and make lasting memories.

To assist with pronunciation, the book includes a dedicated section on Italian grammar and pronunciation rules. This guide will help you develop a basic understanding of the language's structure and provide tips to pronounce Italian words accurately, allowing you to communicate more effectively and confidently.

Lastly, the appendix contains a key vocabulary list, common Italian phrases, and an alphabet and pronunciation guide for quick reference.

These resources serve as a convenient reference point when you encounter unfamiliar words or need assistance in composing your own sentences.

Whether you're a novice language learner or have some prior knowledge of Italian, the Easy Italian Travel Pocket Size Phrase Book is designed to accommodate learners of all levels.

Its clear and concise format, along with practical examples and phonetic spellings, ensures that you can quickly grasp the essentials and engage in meaningful conversations during your Italian adventure.

Now, set off on your journey with confidence, armed with the tools you need to immerse yourself in the enchanting world of Italy.

The Easy Italian Travel Pocket Size Phrase Book is your ultimate companion, empowering you to communicate effortlessly and forge meaningful connections as you explore this captivating country. Buon viaggio! (Have a great trip!)

Basic Italian Expressions: Greetings and Introductions

Hello / Hi - Ciao - "chao" (informal), "chiao" (informal, Southern Italy)

Good morning - Buongiorno - "bwon-JOR-no"

Good afternoon - Buon pomeriggio - "bwon po-meh-REE-joh"

Good evening - Buonasera - "bwona-SEH-ra"

Good night - Buonanotte - "bwona-NOT-te"

How are you? - Come stai? / Come va? - "KO-meh STAI?" / "KO-meh va?"

I'm fine, thank you - Sto bene, grazie - "sto BEH-neh, GRAH-tsyeh"

What's your name? - Come ti chiami? - "KO-meh tee KEE-a-mee?"

My name is... - Mi chiamo... - "mee kee-AH-mo..."

Nice to meet you - Piacere di conoscerti - "pya-CHE-re dee ko-no-SHER-tee"

Goodbye - Arrivederci - "a-ree-ve-DAYR-chee"

See you later - A più tardi / Ci vediamo - "a pyoo TAR-dee" / "che vay-dee-AH-mo"

Please - Per favore - "per fa-VO-re"

Thank you - Grazie - "GRAH-tsyeh"

Excuse me - Mi scusi - "mee SKOO-zee"

How are you doing? - Come va? - "KO-meh va?"

Very well, thank you - Molto bene, grazie - "MOHL-toh BEH-neh, GRAH-tsyeh"

It's nice to see you - È bello vederti - "eh BEL-lo vay-DER-tee"

What is your nationality? - Qual è la tua nazionalità? - "kwahl eh lah TOO-ah na-tsee-oh-nah-LEE-tah"

I'm from [country] - Sono di [paese] - "SO-no dee [PA-eh-zeh]"

How's it going? - Come va? - "KO-meh va?"

Nice to see you again - Piace rivederti - "PYA-chee ree-veh-DER-tee"

What brings you here? - Cosa ti porta qui? - "KO-sa tee POR-ta kwee?"

Have a nice day - Buona giornata - "BWO-na jor-NA-ta"

Have a great weekend - Buon weekend - "BWOHN WEEK-end"

Welcome - Benvenuto / Benvenuta (male/female) - "ben-ve-NOO-toh / ben-ve-NOO-ta"

How long will you stay? - Quanto tempo rimarrai? - "KWOHN-toh TEM-po ree-ma-RYE?"

Are you enjoying your stay? - Ti stai godendo il tuo soggiorno? - "tee STAI go-DEN-do eel TOO-oh soj-JOR-no?"

It's a pleasure to meet you - È un piacere conoscerti - "eh oon pya-CHE-re ko-nos-CHE-rtee"

May I introduce you to... - Posso presentarti a... - "POHs-so pre-zehn-TAR-tee ah..."

Italian Stress Patterns:

In Italian, stress typically falls on the penultimate (second-to-last) syllable if the word ends in a vowel, or on the ultimate (last) syllable if the word ends in a consonant.

The stress patterns for the Italian translations above are indicated in the inverted commas ("") after each word or phrase.

Polite Expressions

Please - Per favore - "per fa-VO-re"

Thank you - Grazie - "GRAH-tsyeh"

You're welcome - Prego - "PREH-go"

Excuse me - Mi scusi - "mee SKOO-zee"

I'm sorry - Mi dispiace - "mee dee-SPYAH-che"

Pardon me - Scusi - "SKOO-zee"

May I help you? - Posso aiutarla? (formal) / Posso aiutarti? (informal) - "POSS-so a-yoo-TAR-la?" / "POSS-so a-yoo-TAR-tee?"

Could you please repeat that? - Potrebbe ripetere, per favore? - "po-TREB-be ree-pe-TE-re, per fa-VO-re?"

Could you please speak more slowly? - Potresti parlare più lentamente, per favore? -

"po-TRES-tee par-LA-re pwee len-TA-men-te, per fa-VO-re?"

I appreciate your help - Apprezzo il tuo aiuto (informal) / Apprezzo il suo aiuto (formal) - "a-PRET-tso eel TOO-oh a-YOO-to" / "a-PRET-tso eel SWOH a-YOO-to"

Excuse me, do you have a moment? - Mi scusi, ha un momento? - "mee SKOO-zee, ah oon mo-MEN-to?"

I apologize for the inconvenience - Mi scuso per l'inconveniente - "mee SKOO-zo per lin-kon-ve-NYEN-te"

May I ask a question? - Posso fare una domanda? - "POSS-so FA-re OO-na do-MAHN-da?"

Could you please help me? - Potrebbe aiutarmi, per favore? - "po-TREB-be a-yoo-TAR-mee, per fa-VO-re?"

I'm sorry, I didn't catch that - Mi scuso, non ho capito - "mee SKOO-zo, non oh ka-PEE-toh"

Please, take your time - Per favore, prenditi tutto il tempo che ti serve - "per fa-VO-re, pren-DEE-tee TOO-toh eel TEM-po kee tee SER-ve"

Thank you very much - Grazie mille - "GRAH-tsyeh MEE-leh"

You're very kind - Lei è molto gentile - "LEH-ee eh MOL-to gen-TEE-leh"

I appreciate your assistance - Apprezzo il suo aiuto - "a-PRET-tso eel SWOH a-YOO-to"

I'm grateful for your support - Sono grato per il tuo sostegno - "SO-no GRA-toh per eel TOO-oh sos-TEG-no"

I beg your pardon - Mi scuso - "mee SKOO-zo"

May I have your attention, please? - Posso avere la vostra attenzione, per favore? -

"POSS-so a-VE-reh lah VOS-tra at-TEN-tsyo-NEH, per fa-VO-re?"

I appreciate your understanding - Apprezzo la vostra comprensione - "a-PRET-tso lah VOS-tra kom-pren-see-OH-neh"

Would you mind if I ask you a favor? - Le dispiacerebbe se le chiedessi un favore? - "le dee-SPYAH-che-REB-be seh le kee-DES-see oon fa-VO-re?"

I'm truly grateful - Sono veramente grato/a - "SO-no veh-rah-MEN-te GRAH-toh/-a"

Thank you for your patience - Grazie per la pazienza - "GRAH-tsyeh per lah pa-TSYEN-tsa"

It's very kind of you - È molto gentile da parte sua - "eh MOL-to gen-TEE-leh da PAR-teh SWAH"

Excuse me for the interruption - Mi scuso per l'interruzione - "mee SKOO-zo per lin-ter-ru-TSYO-ne"

I'm sorry to bother you - Mi dispiace disturbarla - "mee dee-SPYAH-che dis-TOOR-bar-la"

Your assistance is greatly appreciated - La sua assistenza è molto apprezzata - "la SWA a-SEES-TEN-za eh MOL-to a-PRET-tsa-ta"

I would be grateful if you could help me - Sarei grato/a se potesse aiutarmi - "sa-REH-ee GRAH-toh/-a seh po-TES-seh a-yoo-TAR-mee"

Please accept my apologies - Accetti le mie scuse - "a-CHEH-tee le MEE-eh SKOO-zeh"

Thank you for your understanding - Grazie per la comprensione - "GRAH-tsyeh per lah kom-pren-see-OH-neh"

I'm sorry for the inconvenience - Mi dispiace per il disagio - "mee dee-SPYAH-che per eel di-za-GIO"

Your generosity is greatly appreciated - La sua generosità è molto apprezzata - "la SWA ge-ne-ro-SI-ta eh MOL-to a-PRET-tsa-ta"

I sincerely appreciate your help - Apprezzo sinceramente il tuo aiuto - "a-PRET-tso sin-che-re-MEN-te eel TOO-oh a-YOO-to"

May I offer my assistance? - Posso offrirle il mio aiuto? - "POSS-so of-FEER-le eel MEE-oh a-YOO-to?"

Thank you for your cooperation - Grazie per la collaborazione - "GRAH-tsyeh per lah ko-la-bo-ra-TSYO-neh"

I apologize for the misunderstanding - Mi scuso per il malinteso - "mee SKOO-zo per eel ma-lin-TEH-zo"

Your kindness is truly appreciated - La sua gentilezza è veramente apprezzata - "la SWA gen-tee-LET-za eh veh-RA-men-te a-PRET-tsa-ta"

Remember to use these expressions in appropriate situations to convey politeness, gratitude, and sincerity.

Phrases of Appreciation

Thank you - Grazie - "GRAH-tsyeh"

Thanks - Grazie - "GRAH-tsyeh"

I appreciate it - Lo apprezzo - "lo a-PRET-tso"

I'm grateful - Sono grato/a - "SO-no GRAH-toh/-a"

I'm thankful - Sono grato/a - "SO-no GRAH-toh/-a"

I'm really grateful - Sono davvero grato/a - "SO-no da-VVAY-ro GRAH-toh/-a"

I'm so thankful - Sono così grato/a - "SO-no KOS-see GRAH-toh/-a"

I'm deeply grateful - Sono profondamente grato/a - "SO-no pro-fon-da-MEN-te GRAH-toh/-a"

I can't thank you enough - Non ti ringrazierò mai abbastanza - "non tee rin-grat-tsyeh-ROH mai ab-BAS-tan-za"

Your help means a lot to me - Il tuo aiuto significa molto per me - "eel TOO-oh a-YOO-to sig-NEE-fee-ca MOL-to per me"

I'm deeply thankful - Sono profondamente grato/a - "SO-no pro-fon-da-MEN-te GRAH-toh/-a"

I'm extremely grateful - Sono estremamente grato/a - "SO-no es-tre-MA-men-te GRAH-toh/-a"

I'm truly appreciative - Sono sinceramente apprezzativo/a - "SO-no sin-che-ra-MEN-te a-prez-za-TEE-vo/-a"

I'm incredibly thankful - Sono incredibilmente grato/a - "SO-no in-kre-di-BEE-len-te GRAH-toh/-a"

I'm immensely grateful - Sono immensamente grato/a - "SO-no i-men-SA-men-te GRAH-toh/-a"

Thank you from the bottom of my heart - Ti ringrazio dal profondo del cuore - "tee rin-grat-tsyoh dal pro-FON-do del KWO-re"

I'm truly blessed - Sono veramente fortunato/a - "SO-no veh-ra-MEN-te for-tu-NA-to/-a"

I'm grateful beyond words - Sono grato/a oltre le parole - "SO-no GRAH-toh/-a OL-tre le pa-RO-le"

Your support is invaluable - Il tuo sostegno è inestimabile - "eel TOO-oh so-STEG-no eh in-es-ti-MAH-bi-le"

I'm indebted to you - Ti sono debitore/a - "tee SO-no de-BEE-to-re/-a"

I'm so grateful for your kindness - Sono così grato/a per la tua gentilezza - "SO-no KO-si GRAH-toh/-a per la TOO-a gen-tee-LET-za"

Thank you for everything - Grazie per tutto - "GRAH-tsyeh per TOOT-to"

I truly value your help - Apprezzo sinceramente il tuo aiuto - "a-PRET-tso sin-che-re-MEN-te eel TOO-oh a-YOO-to"

You've been incredibly supportive - Sei stato/a di un sostegno incredibile - "sey STAH-toh/-a dee oon so-STEG-no in-kre-di-BEE-le"

I'm thankful for your guidance - Sono grato/a per la tua guida - "SO-no GRAH-toh/-a per la TOO-a GEE-da"

Thank you for your generosity - Grazie per la tua generosità - "GRAH-tsyeh per la TOO-a ge-ne-ro-SI-ta"

Your assistance has been invaluable - Il tuo aiuto è stato prezioso - "eel TOO-oh a-YOO-to eh STAH-to pre-TSYO-zo"

I **deeply appreciate your support** - Apprezzo profondamente il tuo supporto - "a-PRET-tso pro-fon-da-MEN-te eel TOO-oh sor-POR-to"

I'm so lucky to have you - Sono così fortunato/a ad averti - "SO-no KO-si for-tu-NA-to/-a ad a-VER-tee"

Words cannot express my gratitude - Le parole non possono esprimere la mia gratitudine - "le pa-RO-le non po-SON-o es-PREE-me-re lah MEE-a gra-ti-tu-DEE-neh"

Remember to use these expressions genuinely and with a sincere tone to convey your heartfelt appreciation in Italian.

Phrases of Apologizing

Sorry - Scusa/ Mi dispiace - "SKOO-sa/ Mee dees-pee-AH-cheh"

Apologies - Scuse - "SKOO-seh"

I'm sorry - Mi dispiace - "Mee dees-pee-AH-cheh"

Please forgive me - Per favore, perdonami - "Per fa-VO-re, per-do-NA-mi"

I apologize - Mi scuso - "Mee SKOO-so"

Excuse me - Scusa/ Mi scuso - "SKOO-sa/ Mee SKOO-so"

I didn't mean to - Non volevo - "Non vo-LE-vo"

It was my fault - È stata colpa mia - "EH STAH-ta KOL-pa MEE-a"

I take full responsibility - Prendo piena responsabilità - "PREN-do PYE-na re-spon-sa-bee-LEE-ta"

I regret my actions - Mi dispiacciono le mie azioni - "Mee dees-pee-AH-tcho-no le MEE-e a-TSYO-nee"

I'm really sorry - Mi dispiace davvero - "Mee dees-pee-AH-cheh da-VAY-ro"

I apologize for my mistake - Mi scuso per il mio errore - "Mee SKOO-so per eel MEE-o eh-RO-re"

Please accept my apologies - Ti prego di accettare le mie scuse - "Tee PRE-go dee ak-ket-TA-re le MEE-e SKOO-seh"

I didn't mean to offend you - Non volevo offenderti - "Non vo-LE-vo of-fen-DEHR-tee"

I'm deeply sorry for the inconvenience - Mi dispiace molto per l'inconveniente - "Mee dees-pee-AH-cheh MOL-to per lin-kon-ve-NYEN-te"

I regret my words - Mi pento delle mie parole - "Mee PEN-to DEL-le MEE-e pa-RO-le"

I'm truly sorry for my behavior - Mi scuso sinceramente per il mio comportamento - "Mee SKOO-so sin-che-re-MEN-te per eel MEE-o kom-port-A-men-to"

I apologize for any misunderstanding - Mi scuso per qualsiasi fraintendimento - "Mee SKOO-so per kwal-SYA-nyee FRYN-ten-dye-MEN-to"

I'm sorry if I caused any harm - Mi dispiace se ho causato danno - "Mee dees-pee-AH-cheh seh oh kau-ZA-to DAN-no"

I deeply regret my actions - Mi pento profondamente delle mie azioni - "Mee PEN-to pro-fon-da-MEN-te DEL-le MEE-e a-TSYO-nee"

I'm sorry for the misunderstanding - Mi dispiace per il malinteso - "Mee dees-pee-AH-cheh per eel mah-leen-TEH-zo"

Please forgive my mistake - Perdonami per il mio errore - "Per-do-NA-mi per eel MEE-o eh-RO-re"

I apologize for my insensitivity - Mi scuso per la mia insensibilità - "Mee SKOO-so per la MEE-a in-sen-see-bi-lee-TA"

I regret my thoughtless actions - Mi pento delle mie azioni sconsiderate - "Mee PEN-to DEL-le MEE-e a-TSYO-nee skon-shee-ra-teh"

I'm truly sorry for the inconvenience caused - Mi dispiace sinceramente per il disagio causato - "Mee dees-pee-AH-cheh sin-che-re-MEN-te per eel di-za-JO kau-ZA-to"

Please accept my heartfelt apologies - Accetta le mie scuse sincere - "Ach-KET-ta le MEE-e SKOO-seh sin-CHAY-re"

I apologize for any hurt I caused - Mi scuso per qualsiasi dolore causato - "Mee SKOO-so per kwal-SYA-nyee do-LO-re kau-ZA-to"

I'm truly remorseful for my actions - Sono veramente pentito per le mie azioni - "SO-no vay-ra-MEN-te pen-TEE-to per le MEE-e a-TSYO-nee"

I apologize for being thoughtless - Mi scuso per essere stato insensibile - "Mee SKOO-so per es-SER-re STAH-to in-sen-SEE-bi-le"

I'm deeply sorry for my behavior - Mi dispiace profondamente per il mio comportamento - "Mee dees-pee-AH-cheh pro-fon-da-MEN-te per eel MEE-o kom-port-A-men-to"

Feel free to use these phrases to express your apologies in Italian.

Remember to speak sincerely and with genuine remorse.

Phrases for Asking for Help

Help - Aiuto - "Ayu-toh"

Can you help me? - Puoi aiutarmi? - "Pwoi a-yu-tar-mee?"

I need your help - Ho bisogno del tuo aiuto - "O bee-SO-nyo del TOO-oh a-yu-toh"

Please, I need assistance - Per favore, ho bisogno di assistenza - "Per fa-VO-re, o bee-SO-nyo dee a-sis-TEN-za"

Could you lend me a hand? - Potresti darmi una mano? - "Po-TRES-tee DAR-mee OO-na A-no?"

I'm in trouble - Sono nei guai - "SO-no nay GWAH-ee"

I'm lost - Mi sono perso/a - "Mee SO-no PER-so/a"

I don't know what to do - Non so cosa fare - "Non so KO-sa FA-re"

Can you please assist me? - Puoi per favore aiutarmi? - "Pwoi per fa-VO-re a-yu-tar-mee?"

I'm having difficulty - Sto avendo difficoltà - "Sto a-VEHN-do dif-fi-KOL-ta"

Could you please give me a hand? - Potresti per favore darmi una mano? - "Po-TRES-tee per fa-VO-re DAR-mee OO-na A-no?"

I'm struggling with this task - Sto avendo difficoltà con questo compito - "Sto a-VEHN-do dif-fi-KOL-ta kon KWE-sto kom-PEE-to"

Can you show me how to do it? - Puoi mostrarmi come farlo? - "Pwoi moh-STRAHR-mee KO-meh FAR-lo?"

I'm in need of assistance - Ho bisogno di assistenza - "O bee-SO-nyo dee a-sis-TEN-za"

Please, can you help me out? - Per favore, puoi aiutarmi? - "Per fa-VO-re, pwoi a-yu-TAR-mee?"

I'm facing a problem - Sto affrontando un problema - "Sto af-fron-TAN-do oon pro-BLE-ma"

I don't understand - Non capisco - "Non ka-PIS-ko"

Can you explain it to me? - Puoi spiegarmelo? - "Pwoi SPYEH-gar-meh-lo?"

I'm not sure what to do - Non sono sicuro/a di cosa fare - "Non SO-no see-KOO-ro/a dee KO-sa FA-re"

I'm in a difficult situation - Mi trovo in una situazione difficile - "Mee TRO-vo een OO-na see-twa-TSYO-neh dee-fee-CHEE-le"

Can you assist me, please? - Puoi assistere, per favore? - "Pwoi a-SIS-teh-re, per fa-VO-re?"

I'm confused - Sono confuso/a - "SO-no kon-FOO-zo/a"

Could you guide me? - Potresti guidarmi? - "Po-TRES-tee GWEE-dar-mee?"

I'm having trouble understanding - Ho problemi a capire - "O pro-BLE-mee ah ka-PEE-re"

Can you lend me a hand, please? - Puoi prestarmi una mano, per favore? - "Pwoi pres-TAR-mee OO-na A-no, per fa-VO-re?"

I don't know how to proceed - Non so come procedere - "Non so KO-meh pro-CHE-deh-re"

I'm in a bit of a jam - Sono in un bel pasticcio - "SO-no een oon bel pas-TEE-cho"

Could you show me the way? - Potresti indicarmi la strada? - "Po-TRES-tee in-DEE-car-mee la STRA-da?"

I'm struggling with this problem - Sto lottando con questo problema - "Sto lo-TAN-do kon KWE-sto pro-BLE-ma"

Can you offer any assistance? - Puoi offrire un aiuto? - "Pwoi of-FREER-eh oon a-YU-to?"

Asking for Directions

Excuse me, can you help me find...? - Mi scusi, può aiutarmi a trovare...? - "Mee SKOO-zee, pwoh ay-oo-TAHR-mee ah troh-VAH-re...?"

Where is the nearest...? - Dove si trova il più vicino...? - "DO-veh see TRO-va eel pyoo vee-CHEE-no...?"

How do I get to...? - Come si arriva a...? - "KO-meh see ah-REE-vah ah...?"

Is it far from here? - È lontano da qui? - "Eh lon-TAH-no dah kwee?"

Can you show me on the map? - Può mostrarmelo sulla mappa? - "Pwoh moh-STRAR-meh-lo soo-la MAHP-pah?"

Which way should I go? - Quale direzione dovrei prendere? - "KWA-le dee-reh-TSYOH-neh doh-VREY pren-DEH-rey?"

Is there a bus/train that goes to...? - C'è un autobus/un treno che va a...? - "Cheh oon AW-toh-boos/oon TREY-no keh vah ah...?"

Can you give me directions? - Può darmi delle indicazioni? - "Pwoh DAR-mee DEL-le een-dee-ka-TSYOH-nee?"

Where can I find a taxi? - Dove posso trovare un taxi? - "DO-veh POS-so troh-VAH-rey oon TAH-ksee?"

Am I going in the right direction? - Sto andando nella giusta direzione? - "Sto an-DAN-doh NEH-lah JWOOS-tah dee-re-TSYOH-neh?"

Is it close by? - È vicino? - "Eh vee-CHEE-no?"

Can you point me in the right direction? - Puoi indicarmi la giusta direzione? - "Pwoi een-dee-CAR-mee la JWOOS-tah dee-re-TSYOH-neh?"

How far is it? - Quanto dista? - "KWOHN-toh DEES-tah?"

Can you tell me the quickest way? - Puoi dirmi la strada più veloce? - "Pwoi DEER-mee la STRA-da pyoo ve-LO-che?"

Which bus/train should I take? - Quale autobus/treno dovrei prendere? - "KWA-le AW-toh-boos/TREY-no doh-VREY pren-DEH-rey?"

Is there a landmark nearby? - C'è un punto di riferimento nelle vicinanze? - "Cheh oon PUN-toh dee rey-fe-RE-men-to NEHL-les vee-chee-NAHN-tsey?"

Can you repeat that, please? - Puoi ripetere, per favore? - "Pwoi ree-pe-TEH-re, per fa-VO-re?"

Can you draw me a map? - Puoi disegnarmi una mappa? - "Pwoi dee-zay-NAR-mee OO-na MAHP-pah?"

Is it on this street? - È in questa strada? - "Eh een KWE-sta STRA-da?"

Can you show me the way on your phone? - Puoi mostrarmi la strada sul tuo telefono? - "Pwoi moh-STRAR-mee la STRA-da sool TOO-o te-LE-fo-no?"

Excuse me, where is the nearest subway station? - Mi scusi, dov'è la stazione della metropolitana più vicina? - "Mee SKOO-zee, DO-veh lah stah-TSYOH-neh DEHL-lah meh-tro-po-lee-TAH-nah pyoo vee-CHEE-nah?"

Can you recommend a good restaurant around here? - Puoi consigliarmi un buon ristorante qui intorno? - "Pwoi kon-seelyar-mee oon bwon ree-sto-RAN-te kwee een-TOR-no?"

Is there a pharmacy nearby? - C'è una farmacia nelle vicinanze? - "Cheh OO-na far-MA-chee-ah NEHL-les vee-chee-NAHN-tsey?"

Can you help me find the city center? - Puoi aiutarmi a trovare il centro città? - "Pwoi ay-oo-TAR-mee ah troh-VAH-reel CHEN-tro cheet-TAH?"

How do I get to the museum? - Come posso arrivare al museo? - "KO-meh POS-so ar-REE-vah-rey al moo-ZAY-o?"

Where can I buy tickets for the concert? - Dove posso comprare i biglietti per il concerto? - "DO-veh POS-so kom-PRA-rey ee beel-LYET-tee per eel kon-CHER-to?"

Can you tell me where the nearest ATM is? - Puoi dirmi dove si trova il bancomat più vicino? - "Pwoi DEER-mee DO-veh see TRO-va eel BAHN-ko-mat pyoo vee-CHEE-no?"

Is there a tourist information center nearby? - C'è un centro informazioni turistiche nelle vicinanze? - "Cheh oon CHEN-tro een-for-ma-tsyoh-nee too-REE-stee-kee-nehl-les vee-chee-NAHN-tsey?"

How far is the hotel from here? - Quanto dista l'hotel da qui? - "KWOHN-toh DEES-tah LO-tel dah kwee?"

Can you show me the way to the nearest parking lot? - Puoi indicarmi la strada per il parcheggio più vicino? - "Pwoi een-dee-CAR-mee la STRA-da per eel par-KEJ-jo pyoo vee-CHEE-no?"

Transportation

Taxi - Taxi - "TAH-ksi"

Bus - Autobus - "OW-toh-boos"

Train - Treno - "TRE-no"

Metro/Subway - Metropolitana - "Meh-tro-po-lee-TAH-nah"

Tram - Tram - "TRAM"

Airport - Aeroporto - "Ay-eh-ro-POHR-toh"

Port - Porto - "POR-to"

Station - Stazione - "Sta-TSYOH-neh"

Ticket - Biglietto - "Beel-LYET-to"

Schedule - Orario - "O-RA-ryo"

Platform - Binario - "Bee-NA-ryo"

Departure - Partenza - "Par-TEN-za"

Arrival - Arrivo - "A-REE-vo"

Gate - Cancello - "KAN-chehl-lo"

Luggage - Bagaglio - "Bah-GA-lyo"

Rental Car - Auto a noleggio - "OW-toh ah no-LED-jo"

Bicycle - Bicicletta - "Bee-chee-KLEHT-tah"

Motorcycle - Motocicletta - "Mo-to-chee-KLEHT-tah"

Pedestrian - Pedone - "PEH-do-neh"

Traffic - Traffico - "TRAF-fee-ko"

Car - Auto - "OW-toh"

Bicycle - Bicicletta - "Bee-chee-KLEHT-tah"

Motorcycle - Motocicletta - "Mo-to-chee-KLEHT-tah"

Taxi rank - Posteggio dei taxi - "Po-sted-JOH day TAHK-see"

Bus stop - Fermata dell'autobus - "Fer-MAH-tah dell OW-toh-boos"

Train station - Stazione ferroviaria - "Sta-TSYOH-neh feh-roh-vee-AH-ree-ah"

Ticket office - Biglietteria - "Beel-LYET-teh-ree-ah"

Departure board - Tabellone delle partenze - "Ta-bel-LO-neh DEL-leh par-TEN-tseh"

Arrival board - Tabellone degli arrivi - "Ta-bel-LO-neh DEY-lee ah-REE-vee"

Platform number - Numero del binario - "NOO-meh-ro del bee-NA-ryo"

Check-in counter - Banco check-in - "BAN-ko check-in"

Security check - Controllo di sicurezza - "Kohn-TRO-lo dee see-ku-RET-tsa"

Boarding gate - Cancello d'imbarco - "KAN-chehl-lo deem-BAHR-ko"

Baggage claim - Ritiro bagagli - "Ree-TEE-ro bah-GA-lee"

Parking lot - Parcheggio - "Par-KEJ-jo"

Pedestrian zone - Zona pedonale - "ZOH-nah peh-do-NA-leh"

One-way street - Strada a senso unico - "STRAH-dah ah SEHN-soo OO-nee-ko"

Roundabout - Rotatoria - "Ro-tah-TOH-ree-ah"

Traffic jam - Ingorgo stradale - "In-GOR-go stra-DA-leh"

Speed limit - Limite di velocità - "Lee-MEE-teh dee veh-loh-CHEE-tah"

Airport - Aeroporto - "Ah-eh-roh-POHR-toh"

Metro - Metropolitana - "Meh-tro-po-lee-TAH-nah"

Tram - Tram - "Tram"

Ferry - Traghetto - "Trah-GET-toh"

Taxi - Taxi - "TAX-ee"

Rental car - Auto a noleggio - "OW-toh ah noh-LEHD-joh"

Bike rental - Noleggio biciclette - "Noh-LEHD-joh bee-chee-KLEHT-teh"

Pedestrian - Pedone - "Peh-DOH-neh"

Highway - Autostrada - "OW-toh-STRAH-dah"

Bridge - Ponte - "PON-teh"

Intersection - Incrocio - "In-CROH-cho"

Parking - Parcheggio - "Par-KEJ-jo"

Gas station - Stazione di servizio - "Sta-TSYOH-neh dee sehr-VEE-tsyoh"

Traffic light - Semaforo - "Seh-MAH-fa-ro"

Pedestrian crossing - Attraversamento pedonale - "A-tra-ver-SA-men-to pe-do-NA-le"

Bus terminal - Terminal degli autobus - "Ter-MEE-nal DEY-lee ow-toh-BOOS"

Bike lane - Pista ciclabile - "PEES-tah chee-CLA-bee-leh"

Scooter - Motorino - "Mo-to-REE-no"

Helmet - Casco - "KAHS-ko"

These words will come in handy when you are navigating the transportation system in Italy.

Remember to pay attention to the intonations to ensure proper pronunciation.

Buying Tickets

Ticket - Biglietto - "Bee-LYET-toh"

One-way ticket - Biglietto di sola andata - "Bee-LYET-toh dee SOH-la ahn-DAH-ta"

Round-trip ticket - Biglietto di andata e ritorno - "Bee-LYET-toh dee ahn-DAH-ta eh ree-TOHR-no"

Single ticket - Biglietto singolo - "Bee-LYET-toh seen-GOH-lo"

Return ticket - Biglietto di ritorno - "Bee-LYET-toh dee ree-TOHR-no"

Bus ticket - Biglietto dell'autobus - "Bee-LYET-toh del-low-TOH-boos"

Train ticket - Biglietto del treno - "Bee-LYET-toh del TREH-no"

Metro ticket - Biglietto della metropolitana - "Bee-LYET-toh del-lah meh-tro-po-lee-TAH-nah"

Tram ticket - Biglietto del tram - "Bee-LYET-toh del TRAM"

Seat - Posto - "POH-sto"

Reserved seat - Posto prenotato - "POH-sto pre-noh-TAH-to"

Platform - Banchina - "Bahn-KEE-nah"

Departure - Partenza - "Par-TEN-tsah"

Arrival - Arrivo - "Ah-REE-voh"

Schedule - Orario - "O-RAH-ree-oh"

Timetable - Orario dei treni - "O-RAH-ree-oh DEY treh-nee"

Fare - Tariffa - "Tah-REE-fah"

Discount - Sconto - "SKON-to"

Payment - Pagamento - "Pah-gah-MEN-to"

Ticket office - Biglietteria - "Bee-LYET-teh-REE-ah"

Ticket machine - Macchinetta per i biglietti - "Mah-kee-NEHT-tah pehr ee bee-LYET-tee"

Ticket booth - Sportello dei biglietti - "Spor-TEL-lo dey bee-LYET-tee"

Ticket inspector - Controllore dei biglietti - "Kohn-tro-LOH-rey dey bee-LYET-tee"

Validity - Validità - "Vah-lee-DEE-tah"

Expiry date - Data di scadenza - "DAH-tah dee ska-DEN-tsah"

Refund - Rimborso - "Reem-BOR-so"

Exchange - Scambio - "SKAM-bio"

Cancellation - Cancellazione - "Kahn-chel-LAHT-tsioh-neh"

Delay - Ritardo - "Ree-TAHR-doh"

Lost and found - Oggetti smarriti - "O-JET-tee smah-REET-tee"

Platform number - Numero del binario - "NOO-meh-ro del bee-NAH-ree-oh"

Departure time - Orario di partenza - "O-RAH-ree-oh dee par-TEN-tsah"

Boarding pass - Carta d'imbarco - "KAHR-tah deem-BAHR-koh"

Seat reservation - Prenotazione del posto - "Pre-noh-tah-tsee-OH-neh del POH-sto"

Luggage - Bagaglio - "Bah-GAHL-yoh"

Baggage claim - Ritiro bagagli - "Ree-TEE-ro bah-GAH-lee"

Security check - Controllo di sicurezza - "Kohn-TROHL-lo dee see-koo-RET-sah"

Identification - Identificazione - "EE-den-tee-fee-kah-tsee-OH-neh"

Travel insurance - Assicurazione di viaggio - "Ah-see-koo-rah-TSYOH-neh dee VYAH-joh"

Ticket validation - Convalida del biglietto - "Kohn-vah-DEE-dah del bee-LYET-to"

Phrases Used at the Airport

Airport - Aeroporto - "Ah-eh-roh-PORT-oh"

Terminal - Terminal - "Tehr-mee-NAHL"

Departures - Partenze - "Par-TEN-zeh"

Arrivals - Arrivi - "Ah-REE-vee"

Check-in counter - Banco check-in - "BAHN-koh chehk-IN"

Boarding pass - Carta d'imbarco - "KAHR-tah deem-BAHR-koh"

Passport - Passaporto - "Pahs-sah-PORT-oh"

Security check - Controllo di sicurezza - "Kohn-TROHL-lo dee see-koo-RET-sah"

Customs - Dogana - "Doh-GAH-nah"

Baggage claim - Ritiro bagagli - "Ree-TEE-ro bah-GAH-lee"

Flight - Volo - "VOH-loh"

Gate - Cancello - "Kahn-CHEHL-loh"

Boarding - Imbarco - "Eem-BAHR-koh"

Delayed - In ritardo - "Een ree-TAHR-doh"

Canceled - Annullato - "Ah-NOOL-lah-toh"

Connecting flight - Volo di collegamento - "VOH-loh dee kol-leh-gah-MEN-toh"

Baggage - Bagaglio - "Bah-GAHL-yoh"

Lost luggage - Bagaglio smarrito - "Bah-GAHL-yoh smah-REET-toh"

Immigration - Immigrazione - "Ee-mee-grah-TSYOH-neh"

Duty-free shop - Negozio duty-free - "Neh-GO-tsee-oh doo-TEE-free"

Security checkpoint - Punto di controllo di sicurezza - "POON-toh dee kohn-TROHL-lo dee see-koo-RET-sah"

Baggage allowance - Limite del bagaglio - "LEE-mee-teh del bah-GAHL-yoh"

Carry-on luggage - Bagaglio a mano - "Bah-GAHL-yoh ah MAH-noh"

Oversized baggage - Bagaglio fuori misura - "Bah-GAHL-yoh FWOH-ree mee-ZOO-rah"

Customs declaration - Dichiarazione doganale - "Dee-kee-rah-tsyoh-NEH dee-GOH-nah-leh"

Flight attendant - Assistente di volo - "Ah-SEE-sten-teh dee VOH-loh"

Departure gate - Cancello di partenza - "Kahn-CHEHL-loh dee par-TEN-tsah"

Baggage carousel - Nastro trasportatore bagagli - "NAH-stroh trah-spor-tah-TOH-reh bah-GAH-lee"

Airport shuttle - Navetta dell'aeroporto - "Nah-VEHT-tah dell-ah-eh-roh-PORT-oh"

Accommodations: Booking a Hotel

Hotel - Albergo - "AHL-BEHR-goh"

Reservation - Prenotazione - "Preh-noh-tah-TSYOH-neh"

Room - Camera - "KAH-meh-rah"

Check-in - Check-in - "Chehk-EEN"

Check-out - Check-out - "Chehk-AUT"

Reception - Reception - "Reh-SEHP-see-ohn"

Key card - Carta chiave - "KAHR-tah KYAH-veh"

Single room - Camera singola - "KAH-meh-rah SEEN-goh-lah"

Double room - Camera doppia - "KAH-meh-rah DOHP-pyah"

Reservation number - Numero di prenotazione - "NOO-meh-roh dee preh-noh-tah-TSYOH-neh"

Receptionist - Receptionist - "Reh-SEHP-see-oh-nist"

Hotel room - Camera d'albergo - "KAH-meh-rah dahl-BEHR-goh"

Suite - Suite - "SWEET"

Reservation confirmation - Conferma di prenotazione - "Kohn-FEHR-mah dee preh-noh-tah-TSYOH-neh"

Availability - Disponibilità - "Dees-poh-nee-BEE-lee-tah"

Cancellation - Annullamento - "Ah-nool-lah-MEN-toh"

Amenities - Servizi - "Sehr-VEE-tsee"

Breakfast included - Colazione inclusa - "Koh-lah-TSYOH-neh een-KLOO-zah"

Wi-Fi - Wi-Fi - "Wee-FEE"

Concierge - Concierge - "Kon-SYEHRZH"

Front desk - Reception - "Reh-SEHP-see-ohn"

Reservation details - Dettagli della prenotazione - "Deh-TAH-lyee dehl-lah preh-noh-tah-TSYOH-neh"

Room service - Servizio in camera - "Ser-VEE-tsyoh een KA-meh-rah"

Hotel facilities - Servizi dell'hotel - "Ser-VEE-tsyee del-LOH-tehl"

Late check-out - Check-out tardivo - "Chehk-AUT tar-DEE-voh"

Early check-in - Check-in anticipato - "Chehk-EEN an-tee-see-PAH-toh"

Reservation confirmation number - Numero di conferma della prenotazione - "NOO-meh-roh dee kohn-FEHR-mah dehl-lah preh-noh-tah-TSYOH-neh"

Hotel policy - Regolamento dell'hotel - "Reh-goh-lah-MEN-toh del-LOH-tehl"

Deposit - Deposito - "Deh-POH-zee-toh"

Receptionist - Receptionist - "Reh-SEHP-see-ohn-ist"

Check-in time - Orario di check-in - "Oh-RAH-ree-oh dee chehk-in"

Check-out time - Orario di check-out - "Oh-RAH-ree-oh dee chehk-aut"

Single room - Camera singola - "KAH-meh-rah seen-GOH-lah"

Double room - Camera doppia - "KAH-meh-rah DOHP-pyah"

Twin room - Camera con letti singoli - "KAH-meh-rah kohn LEHT-tee seen-GOH-lee"

Suite - Suite - "Sweet"

Hotel amenities - Servizi dell'hotel - "Ser-VEE-tsee del-LOH-tehl"

Room key - Chiave della camera - "KYAH-veh dehl-lah KAH-meh-rah"

Room service - Servizio in camera - "Ser-VEE-tsee een KAH-meh-rah"

Late check-out - Check-out tardivo - "Chehk-aut tar-DEE-vo"

Reception - Reception - "Reh-SEHP-shun"

Lobby - Hall - "Hall"

Restaurant - Ristorante - "Ree-stoh-RAHN-teh"

Bar - Bar - "Bar"

Swimming pool - Piscina - "Pee-SHEE-nah"

Gym - Palestra - "Pah-LEHS-trah"

Spa - Spa - "Spa"

Room service - Servizio in camera - "Ser-VEE-tsee-oh een KAH-meh-rah"

Elevator - Ascensore - "Ah-SHEN-soh-reh"

Parking - Parcheggio - "Par-KEHD-joh"

Business center - Centro business - "CHEN-tro bee-NEHS"

Conference room - Sala conferenze - "SAH-lah kon-feh-REN-tseh"

Laundry service - Servizio lavanderia - "Ser-VEE-tsee-oh lah-vahn-DEH-ree-ah"

Airport shuttle - Servizio navetta per l'aeroporto - "Ser-VEE-tsee-oh nah-VEHT-tah per lah-eh-roh-PORT-oh"

24-hour front desk - Reception 24 ore su 24 - "Reh-SEHP-shun VEN-ti-KWAT-roh-REH soo VEN-ti-KWAT-roh"

Spa and wellness center - Centro benessere e spa - "CHEN-troh ben-ehs-SEH-reh eh spa"

Currency exchange - Cambio valuta - "KAHM-bee-oh vah-LOO-tah"

Luggage storage - Deposito bagagli - "Deh-POH-zee-toh bah-GAH-lee"

Problems and Complaints

Problem - Problema - "Pro-BLEH-mah"

Issue - Problema - "Pro-BLEH-mah"

Complaint - Reclamo - "Reh-KLAH-moh"

I'm not satisfied - Non sono soddisfatto/a - "Non SO-no so-dees-FAH-toh/ah"

The room is not clean - La camera non è pulita - "La KAH-meh-rah non eh poo-LEE-tah"

There is a problem with the air conditioning - C'è un problema con l'aria condizionata - "Cheh oon pro-BLEH-mah kon LAH-ree-ah kohn-dee-tsee-oh-NAH-tah"

The Wi-Fi is not working - Il Wi-Fi non funziona - "Eel Wi-Fi non foon-TSEE-oh-nah"

The shower is not working properly - La doccia non funziona correttamente - "La DOH-tcha non foon-TSEE-oh-nah kor-eh-TEH-mehn-teh"

The noise level is too high - Il livello di rumore è troppo alto - "Eel lee-VEHL-loh dee roo-MOH-reh eh TROHP-poh AHL-toh"

I would like to speak to the manager - Vorrei parlare con il responsabile - "Vor-REH-ee par-LAH-reh kon eel rehs-POHN-sah-bee-leh"

The bed is uncomfortable - Il letto è scomodo - "Eel LET-toh eh skoh-MOH-doh"

There is a leak in the bathroom - C'è una perdita in bagno - "Cheh OO-nah pehr-DEE-tah een BAHN-yoh"

The TV is not working - La televisione non funziona - "La teh-leh-vee-ZYO-neh non foon-TSEE-oh-nah"

The room is too noisy - La camera è troppo rumorosa - "La KAH-meh-rah eh TROHP-poh roo-moh-ROH-sah"

The lights are not functioning - Le luci non funzionano - "Leh LOO-chee non foon-tsee-OH-nah-noh"

The room service is slow - Il servizio in camera è lento - "Eel sehr-VEE-tsee-oh een KAH-meh-rah eh LEHN-toh"

There is a problem with the hot water - C'è un problema con l'acqua calda - "Cheh oon pro-BLEH-mah kon LAH-kwah KAHL-dah"

The air conditioning is too cold - L'aria condizionata è troppo fredda - "Lah-REE-ah kohn-dee-tsee-oh-NAH-tah eh TROHP-poh FREHD-dah"

The room key is not working - La chiave della camera non funziona - "La KYAH-veh DEL-lah KAH-meh-rah non foon-TSEE-oh-nah"

The room was not as advertised - La camera non corrispondeva alla pubblicità - "La KAH-meh-rah non kor-ris-POHN-deh-vah AHL-lah poob-bli-CHI-tah"

There is a strange smell in the room - C'è un odore strano nella stanza - "Cheh oon o-DOH-re STRAH-no neh-lah STAHN-zah"

The room is not clean - La camera non è pulita - "La KAH-meh-rah non eh poo-LEE-tah"

The shower is not functioning properly - La doccia non funziona correttamente - "La DOH-cha non foon-TSEE-oh-nah kor-ret-tah-MEN-teh"

The room was not properly prepared - La camera non era preparata correttamente - "La KAH-meh-rah non EH-rah pre-pa-RAH-tah kor-ret-tah-MEN-teh"

The air conditioning is too noisy - Il condizionatore è troppo rumoroso - "Eel kon-dee-tsee-oh-NA-toh-reh eh TROHP-poh roo-moh-ROH-soh"

There is no hot water in the bathroom - Non c'è acqua calda nel bagno - "Non cheh AHK-wah KAHL-dah nel BAH-nyoh"

The room is too small for our needs - La camera è troppo piccola per le nostre esigenze - "La KAH-meh-rah eh TROHP-poh pee-KOH-lah per leh NOH-streh eh-zee-JEH-neh"

The noise from other guests is disturbing - Il rumore degli altri ospiti è disturbante - "Eel roo-MOH-reh DEH-li AL-tree oh-SPHEE-tee eh dees-toor-BAHN-teh"

The staff is unhelpful - Il personale non è disponibile - "Eel per-soh-NAH-leh non eh dees-poh-NEE-bee-leh"

Dining Out: Ordering Food and Drinks

I would like to order, please. - Vorrei ordinare, per favore. - "Vohr-REH-ee or-DEE-NA-reh, per fah-VOH-reh."

What do you recommend? - Cosa consiglia? - "KOH-sah kohn-SEEL-yah?"

I'm vegetarian/vegan. - Sono vegetariano/vegano. - "SOH-no vay-geh-tah-REE-ah-no/veh-GAH-no."

Can I see the menu, please? - Posso vedere il menù, per favore? - "POHs-so veh-DEH-reh eel meh-NOO, per fah-VOH-reh?"

I would like a table for two. - Vorrei un tavolo per due. - "Vohr-REH-ee oon tah-VOH-loh per DOO-eh."

What is today's special? - Qual è la specialità del giorno? - "KWAH-leh lah speh-chee-ah-LEE-tah del JOHR-no?"

I'll have the steak, please. - Prenderò la bistecca, per favore. - "Prehn-deh-ROH lah beest-EHK-kah, per fah-VOH-reh."

Can I have a glass of water, please? - Posso avere un bicchiere d'acqua, per favore? - "POHs-so ah-VEH-reh oon beek-KYEH-reh DAH-kwah, per fah-VOH-reh?"

Do you have any vegetarian options? - Avete opzioni vegetariane? - "AH-veh-teh ohp-ZEE-oh-nee vay-geh-tah-REE-ah-neh?"

Is the tip included? - È incluso il servizio? - "EH een-CLOO-so eel sehr-VEE-tsee-oh?"

Could I have the menu, please? - Potrei avere il menù, per favore? - "Po-TREH ah-VEH-reh eel meh-NOO, per fah-VOH-reh?"

What do you recommend for dessert? - Cosa consiglia per il dolce? - "KOH-sah kohn-SEEL-yah per eel DOHL-cheh?"

I'm allergic to nuts. - Sono allergico/a alle noci. - "SOH-no ah-lehr-JEE-koh/kah AHL-leh NOH-chee."

Can I have the bill, please? - Posso avere il conto, per favore? - "POHs-so ah-VEH-reh eel KON-to, per fah-VOH-reh?"

Are there any daily specials? - Ci sono delle offerte del giorno? - "Chee SOH-no DEH-leh oh-FEHR-teh del JOHR-no?"

I would like a glass of red wine. - Vorrei un bicchiere di vino rosso. - "Vohr-REH-ee oon beek-KYEH-reh dee VEE-no ROS-so."

Could you please bring me some extra napkins? - Potrebbe portarmi qualche tovagliolo in più, per favore? - "Po-TREB-beh

por-TAHR-mee KWAL-kweh toh-vah-LYO-loh
een PEE-oo, per fah-VOH-reh?"

Is there a vegetarian option for the main course? - C'è un'opzione vegetariana per il piatto principale? - "Cheh oon-ohp-ZYOH-neh vay-geh-tah-REE-ah-nah per eel PYAHT-toh preehn-chee-PAH-leh?"

Do you have any gluten-free dishes? - Avete piatti senza glutine? - "AH-veh-teh PYAHT-tee SEHN-zah GLOO-tee-neh?"

Can I have a cappuccino, please? - Posso avere un cappuccino, per favore? - "POHs-so ah-VEH-reh oon kap-poo-CHEE-no, per fah-VOH-reh?"

I would like to make a reservation for tonight. - Vorrei fare una prenotazione per stasera. - "Vor-REH ee FAH-reh OO-nah preh-noh-TAH-zee-OH-neh per stah-SEH-rah."

Is there a table available for two? - C'è un tavolo disponibile per due? - "Cheh oon TAH-vo-lo dee-SPOH-nee-bee-leh per DOO-eh?"

Could I have a glass of water, please? - Potrei avere un bicchiere d'acqua, per favore? - "Po-TREH ah-VEH-reh oon beek-KYEH-reh DAH-kwah, per fah-VOH-reh?"

Do you have any vegetarian options? - Avete opzioni vegetariane? - "AH-veh-teh OP-zee-OH-nee vay-geh-tah-REE-ah-neh?"

Can I see the dessert menu, please? - Posso vedere il menù dei dolci, per favore? - "POHs-so veh-DEH-reh eel meh-NOO dei DOHL-chee, per fah-VOH-reh?"

Is there a kids' menu available? - C'è un menù per bambini disponibile? - "Cheh oon meh-NOO per bam-BEE-nee dee-SPOH-nee-bee-leh?"

I would like my steak medium-rare. - Vorrei la mia bistecca al sangue. - "Vor-REH la MEE-ah bee-STEH-kah al SAN-gweh."

Is there a house specialty? - C'è una specialità della casa? - "Cheh OO-nah speh-chee-ah-LEE-tah DEL-lah KAH-zah?"

Do you have any gluten-free options? - Avete opzioni senza glutine? - "AH-veh-teh OP-zee-OH-nee SEHN-zah GLOO-TEE-neh?"

Remember to use the appropriate intonation in Italian to convey politeness and clarity when ordering food and drinks. Enjoy your meal!

Asking for the Bill

Can we have the bill, please? - Possiamo avere il conto, per favore? - "Pos-SYAH-mo ah-VEH-reh eel CON-to, per fah-VOH-reh?"

May I have the check, please? - Posso avere il conto, per favore? - "POHs-so ah-VEH-reh eel CON-to, per fah-VOH-reh?"

Excuse me, could we get the bill? - Mi scusi, possiamo avere il conto? - "Mee SKOO-zee, pos-SYAH-mo ah-VEH-reh eel CON-to?"

When you get a chance, could you bring us the bill? - Quando avete un attimo, potreste portarci il conto? - "KWAN-do AH-veh-teh oon aht-TEE-mo, poh-TREH-steh por-TAHR-chee eel CON-to?"

We're ready to pay, could you bring us the bill, please? - Siamo pronti a pagare, potreste portarci il conto, per favore? - "SYAH-mo

PRON-tee ah pah-GAH-reh, poh-TREH-steh por-TAHR-chee eel CON-to, per fah-VOH-reh?"

Excuse me, can I have the bill, please? - Mi scusi, posso avere il conto, per favore? - "Mee SKOO-zee, POHS-so ah-VEH-reh eel CON-to, per fah-VOH-reh?"

Could you bring us the check, please? - Potrebbe portarci il conto, per favore? - "Po-TREB-beh por-TAHR-chee eel CON-to, per fah-VOH-reh?"

We're ready to pay. - Siamo pronti a pagare. - "SYAH-mo PRON-tee ah pah-GAH-reh."

Can you bring the bill, please? - Può portare il conto, per favore? - "POO-oh por-TAH-reh eel CON-to, per fah-VOH-reh?"

May I settle the bill? - Posso pagare il conto? - "POHS-so pah-GAH-reh eel CON-to?"

Restaurant Etiquette

When dining out in a restaurant, it's important to follow certain etiquette guidelines to ensure a pleasant dining experience. Here are some key points to keep in mind:

Reservations: If the restaurant accepts reservations, it's advisable to make one in advance to secure a table, especially during peak hours or for larger groups.

Punctuality: Arrive on time for your reservation or at the agreed-upon time. Being punctual shows respect for the restaurant staff and allows for a smooth dining experience.

Seating: Wait to be seated by the restaurant staff unless otherwise instructed. If you have a preference for indoor or outdoor seating, you can politely request it.

Table Manners: Follow proper table manners, such as keeping your elbows off the table, using utensils appropriately, and chewing with your mouth closed.

Ordering: Be courteous and patient when placing your order. If you have any dietary restrictions or preferences, inform the server politely and inquire about suitable options.

Waitstaff Interaction: Treat the waitstaff with respect and courtesy. Use "please" and "thank you" when requesting items or services, and avoid snapping fingers or using impolite gestures to get their attention.

Mobile Phones: Keep your mobile phone on silent or vibrate mode and avoid talking loudly on the phone while in the restaurant. It's considerate to focus on your dining companions and the dining experience.

Payment: When it's time to settle the bill, review it carefully and calculate any gratuity or service charge if it hasn't been included. Payment methods may vary, but cash and credit cards are typically accepted.

Tipping: In Italy, a service charge is often included in the bill. However, it's customary to leave a small additional tip if the service was exceptional or if the service charge wasn't included.

Dress Code: Some upscale restaurants may have a dress code. It's advisable to dress appropriately for the occasion. If you're unsure about the dress code, you can call ahead or check the restaurant's website for guidance.

Respecting Other Diners: Keep your voice at a moderate level and avoid disturbing other diners. Refrain from using loud or offensive language, and be mindful of personal space.

Special Requests: If you have any specific requests or modifications to the menu items, communicate them politely and clearly to the server.

However, it's important to understand that not all requests may be accommodated due to the restaurant's limitations.

Handling Discrepancies: If there's an issue with your food or service, address it calmly and respectfully with the server or manager. Give them an opportunity to resolve the problem before escalating the situation.

Children's Behavior: If you're dining with children, ensure they are well-behaved and considerate of others. It's helpful to bring activities or distractions to keep them occupied during the meal.

Dietary Restrictions: If you have severe allergies or dietary restrictions, it's crucial to communicate them clearly to the waitstaff.

Inquire about the ingredients and preparation methods to ensure your safety.

Pace of the Meal: In Italy, dining is often a relaxed and leisurely affair. Allow yourself to enjoy the courses at a comfortable pace, and avoid rushing through the meal.

Respect Local Customs: If you're dining in a foreign country, familiarize yourself with any specific cultural customs or norms regarding dining etiquette. This shows respect for the local culture and enhances your overall dining experience.

Saying Goodbye: Before leaving, take a moment to thank the staff for their service and bid farewell. It's a polite gesture that shows appreciation for the dining experience.

Remember, restaurant etiquette is about showing respect, consideration, and appreciation for the dining experience. By adhering to these guidelines, you can ensure a pleasant and enjoyable time at the restaurant.

Basic Shopping Vocabulary

Shop/store - Negozio [neh-GO-zee-oh]

Mall - Centro commerciale [CHEN-troh koh-MEHR-chee-ah-leh]

Market - Mercato [mehr-KAH-toh]

Boutique - Boutique [boo-TEEK]

Department store - Grande magazzino [GRAHN-deh mah-GAHTS-zee-noh]

Cashier - Cassiere/cassiera [kahs-SYEH-reh/kahs-SYEH-rah]

Customer - Cliente [klee-EHN-teh]

Sale - Sconto [SKOHN-toh]

Discount - Sconto [SKOHN-toh]

Price - Prezzo [PREHTS-zoh]

Payment - Pagamento [pah-gah-MEN-toh]

Receipt - Scontrino [skohn-TREE-noh]

Return - Reso [REH-zoh]

Exchange - Cambio [KAHM-byoh]

Size - Taglia [TAHL-yah]

Color - Colore [koh-LOH-reh]

Style - Stile [STEE-leh]

Brand - Marca [MAHR-kah]

Shopping cart - Carrello della spesa [kah-REHL-loh DEHL-lah SPEH-zah]

Shopping bag - Borsa della spesa [BOHR-sah DEHL-lah SPEH-zah]

Cash - Contante [kohn-TAHN-teh]

Credit card - Carta di credito [KAHR-tah dee KREH-dee-toh]

Debit card - Carta di debito [KAHR-tah dee DEH-bee-toh]

Shop assistant - Commesso/commessa [kohm-MEH-soh/kohm-MEH-sah]

Sale - Vendita [VEN-dee-tah]

Discount - Sconto [SKOHN-toh]

Offer - Offerta [oh-FEHR-tah]

Size - Misura [mee-ZOO-rah]

Fit - Vestibilità [ves-tee-bee-LEE-tah]

Try on - Provarsi [proh-VAHR-see]

Cash register - Registratore di cassa [reh-jee-STRAH-toh-reh dee KAHSS-sah]

Display window - Vetrina [veh-TREE-nah]

Salesperson - Venditore/venditrice [ven-DEE-toh/ven-DEE-tree-cheh]

Shopping list - Lista della spesa [LEE-stah DEHL-lah SPEH-zah]

Shopper - Cliente [klee-EHN-teh]

Shoplifting - Taccheggio [tahk-KEH-joh]

Online shopping - Shopping online [SHOHP-peeng ohn-LEEN]

Cash only - Solo contanti [SO-loh kohn-TAHN-tee]

Out of stock - Esaurito [eh-sow-REE-toh]

Sales tax - Imposta sulle vendite [im-POHS-tah SOO-leh VEN-dee-teh]

Department store - Grande magazzino [GRAHN-deh mah-GAHTS-zee-noh]

Market - Mercato [mehr-KAH-toh]

Shopping center - Centro commerciale [CHEN-troh koh-MEHR-chah-leh]

Cashier - Cassiere/cassiera [kahs-SYEH-reh/kahs-SYEH-rah]

Receipt - Ricevuta [ree-CHEH-voo-tah]

Return/exchange - Reso/scambio [REH-zoh/SKAHM-bee-oh]

Shopping bag - Borsa della spesa [BOHR-sah DEHL-lah SPEH-zah]

Price - Prezzo [PREH-tsoh]

Sale - Saldo [SAHL-doh]

Gift - Regalo [reh-GAH-loh]

Window shopping - Fare shopping con la vetrina [FAH-reh SHOHP-peeng kohn lah veh-TREE-nah]

Discounted price - Prezzo scontato [PREH-tsoh SKOHN-tah-toh]

Customer service - Servizio clienti [SEHR-vee-tsyoh KLEE-ehn-tee]

Sales receipt - Scontrino [skohn-TREE-noh]

Cashback - Rimborso in contanti [reem-BOR-soh een kohn-TAHN-tee]

Gift card - Carta regalo [KAHR-tah reh-GAH-loh]

Shop hours - Orari di apertura [OH-rah-ree dee ah-PEHR-tu-rah]

Shopping spree - Follia dello shopping [FOHL-yah DEL-loh SHOHP-peeng]

Shopping cart - Carrello [KAHR-rel-loh]

Colors

Red - Rosso [ROHSS-oh]

Blue - Blu [BLOO]

Yellow - Giallo [JAH-loh]

Green - Verde [VEHR-deh]

Orange - Arancione [ah-rahn-CHOH-neh]

Purple - Viola [VEE-oh-lah]

Pink - Rosa [ROH-zah]

Brown - Marrone [mahr-ROH-neh]

Black - Nero [NEH-roh]

White - Bianco [BYAHN-koh]

Gray - Grigio [GREE-joh]

Silver - Argento [ahr-JEN-toh]

Gold - Oro [OH-roh]

Beige - Beige [BEH-zheh]

Cream - Crema [KREH-mah]

Navy blue - Blu navy [BLOO NAH-vee]

Turquoise - Turchese [toor-KEH-zeh]

Maroon - Vinaccia [vee-NAHCH-ah]

Olive green - Verde oliva [VEHR-deh oh-LEE-vah]

Coral - Corallo [koh-RAHL-loh]

Teal - Turchese scuro [toor-KEH-zeh SKOO-roh]

Lavender - Lavanda [lah-VAHN-dah]

Magenta - Magenta [mah-JEN-tah]

Indigo - Indaco [een-DAH-koh]

Ivory - Avorio [ah-VOH-ree-oh]

Salmon - Salmone [sahl-MOH-neh]

Peach - Pesca [PEH-skah]

Lilac - Lilla [LEE-lah]

Charcoal gray - Grigio carbone [GREE-joh KAR-boh-neh]

Amber - Ambra [AHM-brah]

Bronze - Bronzo [BROHN-tsoh]

Copper - Rame [RAH-meh]

Silver - Argento [ahr-JEN-toh]

Platinum - Platino [plah-TEE-noh]

Pewter - Peltro [PEL-troh]

Rose gold - Oro rosa [OH-roh ROH-zah]

Mauve - Malva [MAHL-vah]

Mint green - Verde menta [VEHR-deh MEN-tah]

Slate gray - Grigio ardesia [GREE-joh ahr-DEH-zee-ah]

Brick red - Rosso mattone [ROH-soh maht-TOH-neh]

Eggshell - Bianco sporco [BYAHN-koh SPOR-koh]

Clothing and Accessories

Shirt - Maglietta [mah-LYET-tah]

Blouse - Blusa [BLOO-zah]

T-shirt - T-shirt [TEE-shert]

Sweater - Maglione [mah-LYOH-neh]

Jacket - Giacca [JAHK-kah]

Coat - Cappotto [kahp-POHT-toh]

Dress - Vestito [ve-STEE-toh]

Skirt - Gonna [GOH-nah]

Pants - Pantaloni [pahn-tah-LOH-nee]

Jeans - Jeans [JEENS]

Shorts - Pantaloncini [pahn-tah-LOHN-chee-nee]

Shoes - Scarpe [SKAHR-peh]

Boots - Stivali [stee-VAH-lee]

Sandals - Sandali [san-DAH-lee]

Sneakers - Scarpe da ginnastica [SKAHR-peh dah jin-nah-STEE-kah]

Hat - Cappello [kahp-PEL-loh]

Cap - Berretto [beh-REH-toh]

Gloves - Guanti [GWAN-tee]

Scarf - Sciarpa [SKEE-AHR-pah]

Belt - Cintura [cheen-TOO-rah]

Socks - Calze [KAHL-tseh]

Underwear - Biancheria intima [bee-ahn-keh-REE-ah een-TEE-mah]

Bra - Reggiseno [rehd-jee-SEH-noh]

Panties - Mutandine [moo-TAHN-dee-neh]

Swimsuit - Costume da bagno [koh-STOH-meh dah BAHN-yoh]

Tie - Cravatta [krah-VAHT-tah]

Bow tie - Farfallino [fahr-fah-LEE-noh]

Handbag - Borsa [BOR-sah]

Wallet - Portafoglio [pohr-tah-FOH-lyoh]

Sunglasses - Occhiali da sole [ohk-KYAH-lee dah SOH-leh]

Watch - Orologio [oh-roh-LOH-joh]

Jewelry - Gioielli [joy-EHL-lee]

Ring - Anello [ah-NEHL-loh]

Necklace - Collana [kohl-LAH-nah]

Earrings - Orecchini [oh-REHK-kee-nee]

Bracelet - Braccialetto [brah-CHYAH-let-toh]

Umbrella - Ombrello [ohm-BREL-loh]

Backpack - Zaino [ZAI-noh]

Suit - Abito [ah-BEE-toh]

Grocery Shopping

Grocery store - Negozio di alimentari [neh-GO-tsyoh dee ah-lee-men-TAH-ree]

Shopping cart - Carrello della spesa [kah-REHL-loh dehl-lah SPEH-zah]

Basket - Cesto [CHEH-stoh]

Aisle - Corsia [KOR-syah]

Produce section - Reparto frutta e verdura [reh-PAHR-toh FROO-tah eh ver-DOO-rah]

Dairy section - Reparto latticini [reh-PAHR-toh lah-tee-CHEE-nee]

Meat section - Reparto carne [reh-PAHR-toh KAR-neh]

Bakery - Panetteria [pah-neht-teh-REE-ah]

Frozen foods - Alimenti surgelati [ah-LEE-men-tee soor-geh-LAH-tee]

Canned goods - Prodotti in scatola [proh-DOHT-tee een skah-TOH-lah]

Bread - Pane [PAH-neh]

Milk - Latte [LAHT-teh]

Eggs - Uova [OO-oh-vah]

Cheese - Formaggio [for-MAH-djoh]

Meat - Carne [KAR-neh]

Fish - Pesce [PEH-sheh]

Fruits - Frutta [FROOT-tah]

Vegetables - Verdure [ver-DOO-reh]

Rice - Riso [REE-zoh]

Pasta - Pasta [PAH-stah]

Snacks - Spuntini [spoon-TEE-nee]

Beverages - Bevande [beh-VAN-deh]

Soda - Bibita gassata [bee-BEE-tah gahs-SAH-tah]

Coffee - Caffè [kah-FEH]

Tea - Tè [TEH]

Bread - Pane [PAH-neh]

Cereal - Cereali [cheh-reh-AH-lee]

Pasta - Pasta [PAH-stah]

Rice - Riso [REE-zoh]

Flour - Farina [fah-REE-nah]

Sugar - Zucchero [ZOO-keh-roh]

Salt - Sale [SAH-leh]

Pepper - Pepe [PEH-peh]

Oil - Olio [OH-lee-oh]

Vinegar - Aceto [AH-cheh-toh]

Condiments - Condimenti [kohn-dee-MEN-tee]

Spices - Spezie [SPEH-tsee-eh]

Cleaning supplies - Prodotti per la pulizia [proh-DOHT-tee pehr lah poo-LEE-tsyah]

Cheese - Formaggio [for-MAH-joh]

Eggs - Uova [WOH-vah]

Butter - Burro [BOOR-roh]

Yogurt - Yogurt [YO-gurt]

Meat - Carne [KAHR-neh]

Poultry - Pollame [pol-LAH-meh]

Seafood - Frutti di mare [FROOT-tee dee MAH-reh]

Frozen food - Cibo surgelato [CHEE-bo soor-geh-LAH-toh]

Canned food - Cibo in scatola [CHEE-bo een skah-TOH-lah]

Baked goods - Prodotti da forno [proh-DOHT-tee dah FOHR-noh]

Sweets - Dolci [DOHL-chee]

Drinks - Bevande [beh-VAN-deh]

Water - Acqua [AHK-kwah]

Juice - Succo [SOOK-koh]

Wine - Vino [VEE-noh]

Souvenirs and Gifts

Souvenir - Souvenir [suh-vuh-NIR]

Gift - Regalo [reh-GAH-loh]

Postcard - Cartolina [kar-toh-LEE-nah]

Keychain - Portachiavi [por-tah-kee-AH-vee]

Magnet - Magnete [MAH-neh-teh]

Scarf - Sciarpa [SHYAHR-pah]

Handbag - Borsa [BOR-sah]

Jewelry - Gioielli [joy-EL-lee]

Perfume - Profumo [proh-FOO-moh]

Artwork - Opera d'arte [OH-peh-rah DAR-teh]

Statue - Statua [STAH-too-ah]

Book - Libro [LEE-broh]

Music CD - CD musicale [seh-DEE moo-zee-KAH-leh]

Local crafts - Artigianato locale [ar-tee-jah-NAH-toh loh-KAH-leh]

Souvenir shop - Negozio di souvenir [neh-GOH-tsee-oh dee soo-vee-NIR]

Gift shop - Negozio di regali [neh-GOH-tsee-oh dee reh-GAH-lee]

Shopping bag - Sacchetto della spesa [sahk-KET-toh DEL-lah SPEH-zah]

Wrapping paper - Carta da regalo [KAHR-tah dah reh-GAH-loh]

Mug - Tazza [TAHT-tsah]

Keyring - Portachiavi [por-tah-kee-AH-vee]

Snow globe - Palla di neve [PAH-lah dee NEH-veh]

Picture frame - Cornice per foto [KOR-nee-cheh per FOH-toh]

Candle - Candela [KAN-deh-lah]

Ornament - Ornamento [or-nah-MEN-toh]

Puzzle - Puzzle [POOT-sleh]

Magnet - Magnete [MAH-neh-teh]

Figurine - Statuetta [stah-TOO-et-tah]

Stationery - Cancelleria [kan-chel-LEH-ree-ah]

Bookmark - Segnalibro [seh-nya-LEE-broh]

Wallet - Portafoglio [por-tah-foh-LYO]

Umbrella - Ombrello [om-BREL-loh]

Local delicacy - Delizia locale [deh-LEE-tsee-ah loh-KAH-leh]

Chocolate - Cioccolato [cho-koh-LAH-toh]

Souvenir magnet - Magnete souvenir [MAH-neh-teh soo-vee-NIR]

Handicrafts - Artigianato [ar-tee-jah-NAH-toh]

Traditional costume - Costume tradizionale [koh-STOO-meh tra-dee-tsee-oh-NAH-leh]

Bargaining and Negotiating

Price - Prezzo [PREHT-zoh]

Discount - Sconto [SKOHN-toh]

Deal - Affare [ahf-FAH-reh]

Offer - Offerta [ohf-FEHR-tah]

Sale - Saldi [SAHL-dee]

Cheaper - Più economico [pyoo eh-koh-NOH-mee-koh]

Expensive - Costoso [koh-STOH-zoh]

Budget - Budget [BOO-jet]

Negotiation - Trattativa [trat-tah-TEE-vah]

Lower the price - Abbassa il prezzo [ahb-BAHS-sah eel PREHT-zoh]

Can you give me a discount? - Puoi farmi uno sconto? [pwoy FAHR-mee OO-no SKOHN-toh]

What's the best price you can offer? - Qual è il miglior prezzo che puoi offrire? [kwahl eh eel MEE-lyor PREHT-zoh keh pwoy ohf-FEER-reh]

I'm on a tight budget - Ho un budget limitato [oh oon BOO-jet lee-mee-TAH-toh]

I'm looking for a good deal - Sto cercando un buon affare [stoh cher-KAHN-doh oon bwon ahf-FAH-reh]

Let's negotiate - Facciamo una trattativa [fah-CHEE-moh OO-nah trat-tah-TEE-vah]

Counteroffer - Controfferta [kohn-troh-FEHR-tah]

Final price - Prezzo finale [PREHT-zoh fah-NEE-leh]

Discounted price - Prezzo scontato [PREHT-zoh skohn-TAH-toh]

Reasonable - Ragionevole [rah-joh-neh-VOH-leh]

Price range - Fascia di prezzo [FAH-shah dee PREHT-zoh]

Compromise - Compromesso [kohm-PROM-ehs-soh]

Worth - Valore [vah-LOH-reh]

I can't afford it - Non posso permettermelo [non POH-soh pehr-MEHT-tehr-meh-loh]

Can we work out a better price? - Possiamo trovare un prezzo migliore? [pohs-SYAH-moh troh-VAH-reh oon PREHT-zoh meel-YOH-reh]

Let's find a middle ground - Cerchiamo un compromesso [chehr-KYAH-moh oon kohm-PROM-ehs-soh]

That's too expensive for me - È troppo costoso per me [eh TROHP-poh koh-STOH-zoh pehr meh]

Is there any room for negotiation? - C'è spazio per una trattativa? [cheh SPAH-tsyoh pehr OO-nah trat-tah-TEE-vah]

Can you make it a bit cheaper? - Puoi renderlo un po' più economico? [pwoy rehn-DEHR-loh oon poh pyoo eh-koh-NOH-mee-koh]

I'm interested, but the price is high - Sono interessato/a, ma il prezzo è alto [SOH-noh in-teh-reh-SAH-toh/a, mah eel PREHT-zoh eh AHL-toh]

Let's discuss the terms - Parliamo delle condizioni [par-LYAH-moh DEH-leh kohn-dzee-OH-nee]

Entertainment and Leisure

Movie - Film [feelm]

Theater - Teatro [teh-AH-troh]

Concert - Concerto [kohn-CHEHR-toh]

Music - Musica [MOO-zee-kah]

Dance - Danza [DAHN-tsah]

Art - Arte [AHR-teh]

Museum - Museo [MOO-zeh-oh]

Exhibition - Mostra [MOH-strah]

Park - Parco [PAR-koh]

Zoo - Zoo [zoh-oh]

Amusement park - Parco divertimenti [PAR-koh dee-ver-tee-MEN-tee]

Sports - Sport [spohrt]

Game - Gioco [JOH-koh]

Swimming - Nuoto [NOO-oh-toh]

Hiking - Escursionismo [ehs-koor-see-oh-NEES-moh]

Beach - Spiaggia [spee-ADJ-ah]

Pool - Piscina [pee-SHEE-nah]

Book - Libro [LEE-broh]

Magazine - Rivista [ree-VEES-tah]

Newspaper - Giornale [jor-NAH-leh]

Music festival - Festival di musica [fes-tee-VAL dee moo-ZEE-kah]

Theater play - Spettacolo teatrale [speh-tah-KOH-loh teh-AH-trah-leh]

Dance performance - Spettacolo di danza [speh-tah-KOH-loh dee DAN-tsah]

Art gallery - Galleria d'arte [gal-LEH-ree-ah DAHR-teh]

Theme park - Parco a tema [PAR-koh ah TEH-mah]

Bowling - Bowling [BOH-ling]

Cycling - Ciclismo [chee-KLEES-moh]

Photography - Fotografia [foh-toh-GRAH-fee-ah]

Concert hall - Sala concerti [SAH-lah kohn-CHEHR-tee]

Outdoor activities - Attività all'aperto [ahk-tee-VEE-tah ahl-lah-PEHR-toh]

Sightseeing and Tourist Attractions

Tours - Visite guidate [vee-ZEE-teh gwee-DAH-teh]

Historical sites - Siti storici [SEE-tee STOH-ree-chee]

Art exhibitions - Mostre d'arte [MOH-streh DAR-teh]

Architecture - Architettura [ar-kee-TEHT-too-rah]

Statues - Statue [STAH-too-eh]

Fountains - Fontane [fohn-TAH-neh]

Theaters - Teatri [TEH-ah-tree]

Concerts - Concerti [kohn-CHEHR-tee]

Festivals - Festival [fehs-tee-VAHL]

Amusement parks - Parchi divertimento [PAR-kee dee-ver-tee-MEN-toh]

Zoos - Zoo [dzo-oh]

Aquariums - Acquari [ah-KWAH-ree]

Botanical gardens - Giardini botanici [jar-DEE-nee boh-tah-NEE-chee]

Observatories - Osservatori [os-ser-va-TOH-ree]

Historical districts - Quartieri storici [kwahr-TYEH-ree STOH-ree-chee]

Landmarks - Luoghi di interesse [LOO-gee dee in-THE-reh-zeh]

Monuments - Monumenti [moh-NOO-men-tee]

Museums - Musei [MOO-zay-ee]

Galleries - Gallerie [gal-LAY-ree-ay]

Parks - Parchi [PAR-kee]

Gardens - Giardini [jar-DEE-nee]

Palaces - Palazzi [pah-LAHTS-ee]

Castles - Castelli [KAHS-teh-lee]

Churches - Chiese [KYEH-zeh]

Cathedrals - Cattedrali [kat-teh-DAH-lee]

Temples - Templi [TEM-plee]

Ruins - Rovine [roh-VEE-neh]

Bridges - Ponti [POHN-tee]

Asking for Recommendations

Recommendations - Raccomandazioni [rah-koh-mahn-dah-TSYOH-nee]

Suggestions - Suggerimenti [soo-jeh-REE-men-tee]

Advice - Consigli [kohn-SEE-lee]

What do you recommend? - Cosa consigli? [KO-zah kohn-SEE-lee]

Can you suggest a good restaurant? - Puoi suggerire un buon ristorante? [pwoy soo-JEH-ree-re oon bwon ree-stoh-RAHN-teh]

Where is a popular tourist attraction? - Dove si trova una famosa attrazione turistica? [DOH-veh see TROH-vah OO-nah fah-MOH-zah ah-trah-TSYOH-neh too-REES-tee-kah]

Any recommendations for shopping? - Qualche raccomandazione per lo shopping? [KWAL-keh rah-koh-mahn-dah-TSYOH-neh per loh SHOH-pee]

What are the must-see places in this city? -
Quali sono i luoghi da non perdere in questa
città? [KWAH-lee SOH-noh ee LOO-oh-ee dah
non PEHR-deh een KWEHS-tah CHEE-tah]

Do you know any good cafes around here? -
Conosci qualche buon caffè qui intorno? [koh-
NOH-shee KWAL-keh bwon kah-FEH kwee
een-TOHR-noh]

Can you recommend a nice hotel? - Puoi
consigliare un bel hotel? [pwoy kohn-see-
LYAH-re oon bel oh-TEHL]

What are the best places to visit? - Quali sono i
posti migliori da visitare? [KWAH-lee SOH-noh
ee POH-stee MEE-lyoh-ree dah vee-ZEE-tah-
re]

Can you suggest a scenic route? - Puoi
suggerire un percorso panoramico? [PWOY

soo-JEH-ree-re oon pehr-KOR-soh pah-noh-
rah-MEE-koh]

Any recommendations for local cuisine? -
Qualche raccomandazione per la cucina
locale? [KWAL-keh rah-koh-mahn-dah-
TSYOH-neh per la koo-CHEE-nah loh-KAH-
leh]

Are there any must-visit attractions nearby? -
Ci sono delle attrazioni da non perdere nelle
vicinanze? [Chee SO-noh DEHL-leh ah-trah-
TSYOH-nee dah non PEHR-deh NEHL-leh
vee-tchee-NAHN-tseh]

Can you suggest a good place for hiking? -
Puoi suggerire un bel posto per fare
escursioni? [PWOY soo-JEH-ree-re oon bel
POH-sto per FAH-reh es-koo-RSYOH-nee]

What's your favorite museum in the city? - Qual
è il tuo museo preferito nella città? [KWAH-leh
eel TOO-oh moo-ZEH-oh preh-feh-REE-to
neh-lah CHEE-tah]

Do you know any off-the-beaten-path attractions? - Conosci delle attrazioni fuori dai percorsi turistici? [Koh-NOH-shee DEHL-leh ah-trah-TSYOH-nee FWOH-ree dye pehr-KOR-see too-rees-TEE-chee]

Can you recommend a good beach to relax? - Puoi consigliare una bella spiaggia per rilassarsi? [PWOY kohn-see-LYAH-re OO-nah BEL-lah SPYAHG-gee-ah per ree-lahs-SAHR-see]

Are there any hidden gems in the area? - Ci sono dei tesori nascosti nella zona? [Chee SO-noh DEH-ee teh-ZOH-ree NAH-sko-stee NEHL-lah ZOH-nah]

Can you suggest a fun activity for families? - Puoi suggerire un'attività divertente per le famiglie? [PWOY soo-JEH-ree-re oon-ah-TTEE-vee dee-ver-TEN-te per leh fah-MEE-lyeh]

Going to the Theater

Theater - Teatro [teh-AH-tro]

Play - Spettacolo teatrale [speh-ttah-KOH-lo teh-AH-trah-leh]

Performance - Performance [per-FOHR-man-cheh]

Actor/Actress - Attore/Attrice [ah-TTOH-reh/ah-TTREE-cheh]

Stage - Palcoscenico [pahl-koh-SHEH-nee-koh]

Ticket - Biglietto [beel-LYEHT-toh]

Box office - Biglietteria [beel-LYEHT-teh-ree-ah]

Curtain - Sipario [see-PAH-ree-oh]

Intermission - Intervallo [in-ter-VAL-loh]

Applause - Applausi [ap-PLAH-oo-zee]

Director - Regista [reh-JEE-stah]

Script - Copione [koh-pee-OH-neh]

Rehearsal - Prova [PROH-vah]

Stage crew - Personale di palcoscenico [pehr-soh-NAH-leh dee pahl-koh-SHEH-nee-koh]

Costume - Costume [koh-STOO-meh]

Props - Oggetti di scena [ohb-JET-tee dee SHEH-nah]

Lighting - Illuminazione [ee-loo-mee-nah-TSYOH-neh]

Sound - Suono [SWOH-noh]

Set design - Scenografia [sheh-noh-GRAH-fee-ah]

Standing ovation - Ovazione in piedi [oh-vah-TSYOH-neh een pyeh-dee]

Sports and Outdoor Activities

Football (soccer) - Calcio [KAHL-chyo]

Basketball - Pallacanestro [pahl-lah-kah-NEHS-troh]

Tennis - Tennis [TEH-nees]

Swimming - Nuoto [NOO-toh]

Cycling - Ciclismo [chee-KLEES-moh]

Hiking - Escursionismo [ehs-koor-see-oh-NEES-moh]

Running - Corsa [KOR-sah]

Skiing - Sci [skee]

Surfing - Surf [soorf]

Camping - Campeggio [kam-PEH-joh]

Golf - Golf [golf]

Volleyball - Pallavolo [pahl-lah-VOH-loh]

Baseball - Baseball [baseball]

Horse riding - Equitazione [eh-kwee-tah-TSYOH-neh]

Surfing - Surf [soorf]

Sailing - Vela [VEH-lah]

Fishing - Pesca [PEHS-kah]

Yoga - Yoga [YO-gah]

Rock climbing - Arrampicata [ah-rahm-pee-KAH-tah]

Scuba diving - Immersioni subacquee [ee-mehr-see-OH-nee soo-BAHK-weh]

Health and Emergencies

Doctor - Medico [MEH-dee-koh]

Hospital - Ospedale [oh-speh-DAH-leh]

Pharmacy - Farmacia [fahr-MAH-chyah]

Emergency - Emergenza [eh-mehr-JEN-tsah]

Ambulance - Ambulanza [ahm-boo-LAHN-tsah]

Police - Polizia [poh-LEE-tsyah]

Fire - Incendio [een-CHEHN-dyoh]

Accident - Incidente [een-CHEE-den-teh]

Pain - Dolore [DOH-loh-reh]

Fever - Febbre [FEHB-breh]

Injury - Lesione [leh-ZYO-neh]

Illness - Malattia [mah-LAHT-tee-yah]

Allergy - Allergia [ahl-LEHR-jee-yah]

Medicine - Medicina [meh-dee-CHEE-nah]

Bandage - Benda [BEHN-dah]

CPR - Rianimazione cardiopolmonare [ree-ah-nee-mah-zee-OH-neh   kar-dee-oh-pohl-MOH-nah-reh]

Headache - Mal di testa [mahl dee TEH-stah]

Stomachache - Mal di stomaco [mahl dee stoh-MAH-koh]

Breathing difficulties - Difficoltà respiratorie [dee-fee-KOHL-tah reh-spee-rah-TOH-ree-eh]

Emergency room - Pronto soccorso [PROHN-toh sok-KOHR-soh]

Cough - Tosse

Sore throat - Mal di gola

Nausea - Nausea

Cold - Raffreddore

Toothache - Mal di denti

Back pain - Mal di schiena

Joint pain - Dolore alle articolazioni

Earache - Mal d'orecchio

Sinus congestion - Congestione dei seni nasali

Sore muscles - Muscoli doloranti

Fatigue - Affaticamento

Insomnia - Insonnia

Rash - Eruzione cutanea

Sunburn - Scottatura solare

Dehydration - Disidratazione

Diarrhea - Diarrea

Cough - Tosse

Flu – Influenza

Pharmacy - Farmacia [far-ma-CHI-a]

Medication - Medicinale [me-di-ci-NA-le]

Prescription - Ricetta medica [ri-CET-ta ME-di-ca]

Pill - Pillola [pi-LO-la]

Tablet - Compressa [com-PRES-sa]

Capsule - Capsula [ca-PU-la]

Syrup - Sciroppo [sci-ROP-po]

Cream - Crema [CRE-ma]

Ointment - Unguento [un-GUEN-to]

Drops - Gocce [GOC-ce]

Antibiotic - Antibiotico [an-ti-bio-TI-co]

Painkiller - Antidolorifico [an-ti-do-lo-RI-fi-co]

Antihistamine - Antistaminico [an-ti-sta-MI-ni-co]

Prescription refill - Rinnovo della ricetta [rin-NO-vo DEL-la ri-CET-ta]

Over-the-counter - Senza prescrizione [SEN-za pre-scri-ZIO-ne]

Prescription - Prescrizione [pres-cri-ZIO-ne]

Medication - Medicinale [me-di-ci-NA-le]

X-ray - Radiografia [ra-di-o-GRA-fi-a]

Blood test - Esame del sangue [e-SA-me del SAN-gue]

Medical insurance - Assicurazione medica [as-si-cu-ra-ZIO-ne ME-di-ca]

Symptoms - Sintomi [SIN-to-mi]

Diagnosis - Diagnosi [dia-GNO-si]

Treatment - Trattamento [tra-tta-MEN-to]

Remember to seek immediate medical attention in case of emergencies or serious health concerns. It's also important to communicate with healthcare professionals who can provide accurate guidance and support for your specific medical needs.

Time and Numbers

Time - Ora [O-ra]

Clock - Orologio [o-ro-LO-gio]

Hour - Ora [O-ra]

Minute - Minuto [mi-NU-to]

Second - Secondo [se-CO-n-do]

Morning - Mattina [mat-TI-na]

Afternoon - Pomeriggio [po-me-RIG-gio]

Evening - Sera [SE-ra]

Night - Notte [NOT-te]

Midnight - Mezzanotte [mez-za-NOT-te]

Half past - E mezzo [e MEL-zo]

Quarter past - E un quarto [e un QUAR-to]

Quarter to - Meno un quarto [ME-no un QUAR-to]

AM - AM (Antimeridiano) [an-ti-me-ri-DIA-no]

PM - PM (Postmeridiano) [post-me-ri-DIA-no]

Watch - Orologio da polso [o-ro-LO-gio da POL-so]

Digital - Digitale [di-gi-TA-le]

Analog - Analogico [a-no-LO-gi-co]

Hour hand - Lancetta delle ore [lan-CET-ta DEL-le O-re]

Minute hand - Lancetta dei minuti [lan-CET-ta dei mi-NU-ti]

Second hand - Lancetta dei secondi [lan-CET-ta dei se-CON-di]

Time zone - Fuso orario [FU-so o-RA-rio]

Daytime - Diurno [di-UR-no]

Nighttime - Notturno [not-TUR-no]

Past - Passato [pas-SA-to]

To - A [a]

Early - Presto [PRES-to]

Late - Tardi [TAR-di]

Duration - Durata [du-RA-ta]

Stopwatch - Cronometro [cro-NO-me-tro]

Days of the Week

Monday - Lunedì [lu-NE-di]

Tuesday - Martedì [mar-TE-di]

Wednesday - Mercoledì [mer-co-LE-di]

Thursday - Giovedì [gio-VE-di]

Friday - Venerdì [ve-NE-ri]

Saturday - Sabato [SA-ba-to]

Sunday - Domenica [do-ME-ni-ca]

Months of the Year

January - Gennaio [jen-NA-yo]

February - Febbraio [feb-BRA-yo]

March - Marzo [MAR-tso]

April - Aprile [A-pri-le]

May - Maggio [MADJ-jo]

June - Giugno [JU-njo]

July - Luglio [LU-lyo]

August - Agosto [a-GOS-to]

September - Settembre [set-TEM-bre]

October - Ottobre [ot-TO-bre]

November - Novembre [no-VEM-bre]

December - Dicembre [di-CEM-bre]

Seasons of the Year

Spring - Primavera [pri-ma-VE-ra]

Summer - Estate [e-STAH-te]

Autumn/Fall - Autunno [au-TUN-no]

Winter - Inverno [in-VER-no]

Currency

Money - Denaro [de-NA-ro]

Cash - Contante [con-TAN-te]

Euro - Euro [E-u-ro]

Dollar - Dollaro [dol-LA-ro]

Cent - Centesimo [chen-TE-zi-mo]

Banknote - Banconota [ban-ko-NO-ta]

Coin - Moneta [mo-NE-ta]

Exchange rate - Tasso di cambio [TAS-so dee CAM-bio]

ATM - Bancomat [ban-ko-MAT]

Credit card - Carta di credito [CAR-ta dee CRE-di-to]

Bank - Banca [BAN-ca]

Account - Conto [CON-to]

Savings - Risparmi [ris-PAR-mi]

Withdrawal - Prelievo [pre-LIE-vo]

Deposit - Deposito [de-PO-zi-to]

Balance - Saldo [SAL-do]

Currency exchange - Cambio valuta [CAM-bio va-LU-ta]

Traveler's checks - Assegni viaggio [as-SEG-ni vya-GGIO]

Wallet - Portafoglio [por-ta-fo-LIO]

Receipt - Scontrino [scon-TRI-no]

Numbers

Zero - Zero [ZEH-ro]

One - Uno [OO-no]

Two - Due [DOO-eh]

Three - Tre [TREH]

Four - Quattro [KWA-tro]

Five - Cinque [CHEEN-kweh]

Six - Sei [SEH-ee]

Seven - Sette [SET-teh]

Eight - Otto [OT-to]

Nine - Nove [NO-veh]

Ten - Dieci [DYEH-chee]

Eleven - Undici [OON-dee-chee]

Twelve - Dodici [DOH-dee-chee]

Thirteen - Tredici [TREH-dee-chee]

Fourteen - Quattordici [KWA-tor-DEE-chee]

Fifteen - Quindici [KWIN-dee-chee]

Sixteen - Sedici [SEH-dee-chee]

Seventeen - Diciassette [dee-CHAS-set-teh]

Eighteen - Diciotto [dee-CHO-to]

Nineteen - Diciannove [dee-CHAHN-no-veh]

Twenty - Venti [VEN-tee]

Thirty - Trenta [TREN-ta]

Forty - Quaranta [kwa-RAN-ta]

Fifty - Cinquanta [cheen-KWAN-ta]

Sixty - Sessanta [ses-SAN-ta]

Seventy - Settanta [set-TAN-ta]

Eighty - Ottanta [ot-TAN-ta]

Ninety - Novanta [no-VAN-ta]

One hundred - Cento [CHEN-to]

One thousand - Mille [MIL-leh]

One million - Un milione [oon mee-LYOH-neh]

One billion - Un miliardo [oon mee-LEE-ar-do]

Grammar and Pronunciation Guide

English - Inglese [in-GLEH-zeh]

Grammar - Grammatica [gra-MAH-tee-cah]

Pronunciation - Pronuncia [pro-NOON-see-ah]

Nouns - Sostantivi [so-stan-TEE-vee]

Verbs - Verbi [VER-bee]

Adjectives - Aggettivi [a-jet-TEE-vee]

Adverbs - Avverbi [av-VER-bee]

Prepositions - Preposizioni [pre-po-ZEE-tsee-oh-nee]

Conjunctions - Congiunzioni [kon-joo-NZYO-nee]

Articles - Articoli [ar-TEE-koh-lee]

Present Tense - Presente [pre-ZEN-teh]

Past Tense - Passato [pa-SAH-toh]

Future Tense - Futuro [foo-TOO-roh]

Imperative - Imperativo [im-pe-RAH-tee-vo]

Singular - Singolare [sin-GO-lah-reh]

Plural - Plurale [plu-RAH-leh]

Subject - Soggetto [soj-GET-toh]

Object - Oggetto [o-GGET-toh]

Verb - Verbo [VER-bo]

Adjective - Aggettivo [a-jet-TEE-vo]

Adverb - Avverbio [av-VER-bee]

Subject Pronouns - Pronomi personali [pro-NO-mee per-so-NAH-lee]

Possessive Pronouns - Pronomi possessivi [pro-NO-mee po-ses-SEE-vee]

Reflexive Pronouns - Pronomi riflessivi [pro-NO-mee ree-FLES-see-vee]

Demonstrative Pronouns - Pronomi dimostrativi [pro-NO-mee dee-mos-TRA-tee-vee]

Interrogative Pronouns - Pronomi interrogativi [pro-NO-mee in-ter-ro-GA-tee-vee]

Subject-Verb Agreement - Concorda tra soggetto e verbo [kon-KOR-da tra soj-GET-toh e VER-bo]

Sentence Structure - Struttura della frase [stroo-TOO-ra del-la FRAH-ze]

Word Order - Ordine delle parole [or-DEE-ne DEL-le pa-RO-le]

Pronunciation Tips - Suggerimenti di pronuncia [soo-ger-EE-men-tee dee pro-NOON-see-ah]

Stress - Accento [ak-KEN-toh]

Intonation - Intonazione [in-toh-na-TSYOH-neh]

Phonetics - Fonetica [fo-NE-tee-cah]

Syntax - Sintassi [sin-TAH-see]

Sentence - Frase [FRAH-zeh]

Phrase - Espressione [es-pre-see-OH-neh]

Clause - Clausola [KLAH-oo-zoh-lah]

Subject - Soggetto [soj-GET-toh]

Predicate - Predicato [pre-di-KAH-toh]

Object - Oggetto [o-GGET-toh]

Noun - Nome [NO-meh]

Preposition - Preposizione [pre-po-see-TSYOH-neh]

Conjunction - Congiunzione [kon-joo-NZYO-neh]

Definite Article - Articolo determinativo [ar-TEE-koh-lo de-ter-mee-NAH-tee-vo]

Indefinite Article - Articolo indeterminativo [ar-TEE-koh-lo in-de-ter-mee-NAH-tee-vo]

Possessive Pronouns - Pronomi possessivi [pro-NO-mee po-ses-SEE-vee]

Reflexive Pronouns - Pronomi riflessivi [pro-NO-mee ree-FLES-see-vee]

Interrogative Pronouns - Pronomi interrogativi [pro-NO-mee in-ter-ro-GA-tee-vee]

Demonstrative Pronouns - Pronomi dimostrativi [pro-NO-mee dee-mos-TRA-tee-vee]

Relative Pronouns - Pronomi relativi [pro-NO-mee re-la-TI-vee]

Conditional - Condizionale [kon-dee-tsyoh-NAH-leh]

Imperative - Imperativo [im-pe-RAH-tee-vo]

Gerund - Gerundio [ge-RUN-dee-oh]

Participle - Participio [par-TEE-CHEE-po]

Pronunciation Guide

A (/æ/) - pronounced like the "a" in "cat" - simile a "a" in "gatto"

E (/iː/) - pronounced like the "ee" in "tree" - simile a "i" in "albero"

I (/aɪ/) - pronounced like the "ai" in "rain" - simile a "ai" in "pioggia"

O (/oʊ/) - pronounced like the "o" in "go" - simile a "o" in "andare"

U (/juː/) - pronounced like the "oo" in "moon" - simile a "u" in "luna"

R (/r/) - rolled "r" sound - suono "r" arrotolato

TH (/θ/ and /ð/) - pronounced like the "th" in "think" and "that" - simile a "th" in "pensare" e "quello"

SH (/ʃ/) - pronounced like the "sh" in "she" - simile a "sh" in "lei"

CH (/tʃ/) - pronounced like the "ch" in "chair" - simile a "ch" in "sedia"

J (/dʒ/) - pronounced like the "j" in "jump" - simile a "j" in "saltare"

Remember that pronunciation can vary based on regional accents, so it's always helpful to listen to native speakers and practice your pronunciation with them.

Alphabet and Pronunciation Guide

A - [ah]

B - [bee]

C - [chee]

D - [dee]

E - [eh]

F - [effe]

G - [gee]

H - [acca]

I - [ee]

L - [elle]

M - [emme]

N - [enne]

O - [oh]

P - [pee]

Q - [ku]

R - [erre]

S - [esse]

T - [tee]

U - [oo]

V - [vee]

Z - [zee]

Please note that the pronunciation of some letters may vary depending on their position in a word and the surrounding letters.

Additionally, it's important to note a few pronunciation rules in Italian:

Every letter is pronounced, and there are no silent letters.

Vowels are generally pronounced in a pure form, without diphthongs.

Double consonants are pronounced with a slightly longer duration than single consonants.

Stress usually falls on the penultimate syllable, unless there is an accent mark indicating otherwise.

Practice listening to and repeating Italian words to familiarize yourself with the correct pronunciation. It may also be helpful to use online pronunciation guides or language-learning resources to refine your pronunciation skills.

Printed in Great Britain
by Amazon

39080297R00086